S0-AGM-003

HORSING AROUND

SHETLAND PONIES

By Kristen Rajczak

Gareth Stevens
Publishing

Please visit our website, www.garethstevens.com. For a free color catalog of all our high-quality books, call toll free 1-800-542-2595 or fax 1-877-542-2596.

Library of Congress Cataloging-in-Publication Data

Rajczak, Kristen.
Shetland ponies / Kristen Rajczak.
    p. cm. — (Horsing around)
Includes index.
ISBN 978-1-4339-6474-9 (pbk.)
ISBN 978-1-4339-6475-6 (6-pack)
ISBN 978-1-4339-6472-5 (library binding)
1. Shetland pony. I. Title.
SF315.2.S5R35 2012
636.1′6—dc23

                                                2011019303

First Edition

Published in 2012 by
Gareth Stevens Publishing
111 East 14th Street, Suite 349
New York, NY 10003

Designer: Michael J. Flynn
Editor: Therese Shea

Photo credits: Cover, p. 1 iStockphoto; (cover, back cover, p. 1 wooden sign), (front cover, back cover, pp. 2–4, 7–8, 11–12, 15–16, 19–24 wood background), 5, 6, 9 (all), 10, 14, 18, 20, 21 Shutterstock.com; p. 13 Charles Hewitt/Hulton Archive/Getty Images; p. 17 Michael C. Gray/ Shutterstock.com.

Printed in the United States of America

CPSIA compliance information: Batch #CW12GS: For further information contact Gareth Stevens, New York, New York at 1-800-542-2595.

Contents

e used in the text.

Have you ever ridden a pony? Ponies are small horses. They're under 57 inches (145 cm) tall at the **withers**. Horse lovers might say they're 14.2 **hands** high. Ponies look a bit different from other horses. They usually have shorter legs and a thicker coat and mane.

The Shetland pony is one of the most popular pony **breeds**. Though Shetland ponies were working horses in the past, many people today keep them as pets. Shetland ponies have a sweet nature and are good with children.

Ponies, such as this Shetland pony, can be called horses. But not all horses can be called ponies!

The size difference between a Shetland pony and other horses is clearly shown in this photo.

Standing Small

The Shetland pony is the second-smallest horse breed. Unlike most horses, Shetland ponies aren't measured in hands. Most are only about 40 inches (102 cm) tall at the withers. They weigh between 330 and 440 pounds (150 and 200 kg).

Shetland ponies have short, strong legs. Their middle is round with a short, wide back. They have small heads with friendly faces and rounded, forward-pointing ears. Their eyes can be many different colors.

THE MANE FACT

The miniature horse is the smallest horse breed. "Miniature" means "very small."

Colorful Coat

Shetland ponies can be many colors, including black, gray, and a reddish-brown color called chestnut. Some have spots called dapples. A Shetland pony's mane and tail are full and long. Its coat is very thick.

Shetland ponies have thick coats because of where their **ancestors** came from. Early Shetland ponies lived on islands north of Scotland. The land was rocky, and the weather conditions were rough. Shetland ponies' shaggy coats helped **protect** them from the cold, wind, and rain.

THE MANE FACT

Shetland pony parents pass on the color or colors of their coats to their children.

With so many possible coat colors, Shetland ponies all look different and special.

Shetland ponies can still be found in Scotland today.

Shetland ponies got their name from their island homes—the Shetland Islands. No one knows how the breed started. However, it's thought that travelers to the islands brought horses that became the ponies' ancestors. These may have included Arabian horses and larger ponies.

The people of the Shetland Islands used the small, strong ponies to pull heavy loads of **peat** and seaweed. Peat was burned for warmth. Seaweed helped crops grow. The ponies made the people's lives easier.

THE MANE FACT

Shetland ponies can pull twice their own weight!

Pony of the Coal Mines

During the 1800s, many Shetland ponies were sent to work in England's coal **mines**. They pulled carts full of coal around the mines. Their small size and great strength made them good for the job. Many Shetland ponies were born in the mines and died in them, too. Some ponies were taken to the United States in the 1880s to work in the coal mines.

By the mid-1900s, machines had taken over the ponies' jobs. Today, some Shetland ponies still pull heavy carts in weight-pulling events at fairs.

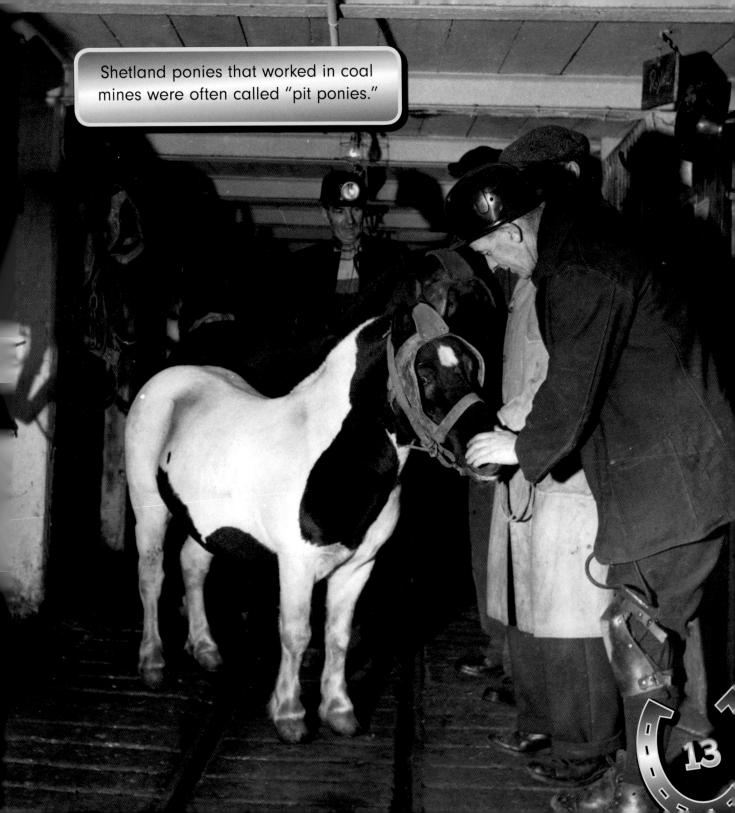

Shetland ponies that worked in coal mines were often called "pit ponies."

13

Shetland pony owners often teach their ponies to be riding horses.

14

The rough conditions on the Shetland Islands and the work in the mines made the Shetland pony breed **hardy**. Early ponies passed on their tough qualities and strong bodies to their children. Today's Shetland ponies can work for a long time. They can also play a long time!

Shetland ponies make good companions and pets. They're usually gentle. Shetland ponies are friendly to children and other animals. They're also smart and learn quickly. This makes Shetland ponies easy to train.

THE MANE FACT

Many horseback riders got their start riding Shetland ponies.

Types of Shetland Ponies

There are several types of Shetland ponies. Foundation Shetland ponies look much like the early ponies from the Shetland Islands. Classic Shetland ponies are thought to have the best features of their ancestors. Modern Shetland ponies have the beauty of the Classic Shetland pony and the **energy** of another small breed called the Hackney pony. American show ponies are larger than Modern Shetland ponies. They can have Shetland pony or Hackney pony parents. The National show pony has one **purebred** Shetland pony or miniature horse parent.

Ponies in horse shows often can't be taller than a certain height.

17

Other horse breeds might be too big for this little girl to ride, but a Shetland pony is just right.

Shetland ponies have worked with people for hundreds of years. Today, some Shetland ponies train to become guide horses. They lead those who can't see well. Guide horses help their owners through crowds and may even go on subways and buses!

Shetland ponies are often used for horseback riding. They're gentler than many full-size horses. In fact, they're the perfect size for children who are learning to ride horses.

THE MANE FACT

In order to enter a Shetland pony in a horse show, owners must know what type they have.

19

A Shetland pony is a wonderful addition to a family. The ponies live a long time and don't need a lot of care. However, even though Shetland ponies are small, owning a horse is a big job.

The ponies need training so they keep out of trouble. It's also important for them to have a large area to move around in and a safe, warm, dry place to sleep. When they're well cared for, Shetland ponies are lots of fun!

Height
32 to 46 inches
(81 to 117 cm) at the withers

Weight
330 to 440 pounds
(150 to 200 kg)

Shetland
Pony Facts

Colors
many, including black,
chestnut, and gray

Life Span
20 to 25 years

Glossary

ancestor: someone who lived before others in a family

breed: a group of animals that share features different from other groups of the kind

energy: the condition of being full of life

hand: a measurement used for a horse's height. One hand equals 4 inches (10.2 cm).

hardy: able to withstand poor conditions

mine: a pit or tunnel from which rocks and other matter are taken

peat: the matter left over from plants that have partly broken down in water

protect: to keep safe

purebred: an animal that has family members of only one breed

withers: the area between a horse's shoulder bones

Books

Monahan, Erin. *Shetland Ponies*. Mankato, MN: Capstone Press, 2009.

Ransford, Sandy. *At the Show*. Mankato, MN: QEB Publishing, 2012.

Rumsch, BreAnn. *Shetland Ponies*. Edina, MN: ABDO Publishing, 2011.

Websites

All About Horses
www.darley.co.uk/darleykids/all-about-horses/
Read about horses' bodies and what they eat.

Horse Breed Directory: Shetland Pony
animal.discovery.com/guides/horses/breeds/shetland.html
Learn more about the Shetland pony and other horse breeds.

Index